Becoming The Narcissist's Nightmare in Sixty (60) Minutes

Master the Art of Overcoming the Narcissist and Healing from Narcissistic Abuse

Jeremy Gaines

Copyright Statement

Acknowledgement

First and foremost, I would like to express my heartfelt gratitude to God for the grace and strength he bestowed upon me to bring the writing of this book to fruition. There were so many hurdles I had to break in order to write this book, but for his unfailing grace, I couldn't have come this far. Thank you Lord!

Special thanks goes to Faith Gaines for her tireless support and love she has shown towards me. Hailing from Chicago-Illinois. Faith is a devout Christian, a Prophetess, philanthropist, a counselor and a cynosure of God's unfailing love. She is a sister, a mother, an auntie and a friend to me. She is among a few people who convinces me good people still exist.

The Lord has used this woman of God to affect my life both spiritually and physically as well as others in Ghana and

Overseas. In case you didn't know, one of my greatest inspirations to write this book came from God through her and I am so grateful for this. I think I would have to write another book just to mention the support she has shown towards God's work and many lives. Thank you so much.

A big thank you to Prophet Kingsley Arthur (Logos Son) for the untiring devotion and support he has shown towards me ever since I knew him. Kinsley has been a son to me since High School, his humility and desire to learn has always left me in awe. He has ceaselessly stood in prayer from day one to support me and I can't thank God enough for such a blessing as this.

I extend my deepest appreciation to my mentor and advisors who have generously shared their wisdom, expertise, and guidance. Their valuable insights, constructive criticism, and commitment to excellence have been instrumental in shaping this work into its final form.

Finally, I want to express my gratitude to the readers who have chosen to embark on this literary journey with me. Your engagement, support, and feedback are truly appreciated, and it is my sincerest hope that this book provides you with insights, hope, and a thought-provoking experience to enter into a new realm of transformation.

To all those who have played a role, big or small, in the creation of this book, I extend my heartfelt appreciation and gratitude.

Thank you.

Jeremy Gaines.

Table of content

Acknowledgement 3

CHAPTER 1 11

Who is a Narcissist? 11

How narcissists are formed 12

CHAPTER 2 18

The Narcissist's Target 18

CHAPTER 3 22

The Biochemical Bonds That Get Us "Hooked" On Narcissists
.... 22

CHAPTER 4 25

How to know You Have Suffered Narcissistic abuse 25

Childhood Programming that makes you a Magnet for
Narcissists 28

CHAPTER 5 34

Where can the narcissist be found? 34

The workplace Narcissist 36

The religious Narcissists. 39

Some common behaviors associated with religious
narcissism include 43

Romantic relationships 45

Family 47

Political Narcissists 49

CHAPTER 6 54

Types of Narcissists 54

CHAPTER 7 82

Victims' Emotional and Psychological Reasons for Staying in Narcissistic Abuse 82

CHAPTER 8 86

The Antidote 86

CHAPTER 9 106

Therapeutic Approaches for dealing with Narcissistic abuse. 106

CHAPTER 10 112

Closing Thoughts 112

Reference 116

Introduction

" Becoming The Narcissist's Nightmare in Sixty Minutes" is a riveting and enlightening concise book that sheds a spotlight on the mentality of a narcissist and the destructive impact their actions can have on people around them. This book gives a complete guide for anybody who has experienced a narcissistic individual in their personal or professional life, and attempts to understand and overcome the destructive influence of such persons. Written in a brief and easy-to-read manner, this book gives practical ideas and techniques for dealing with narcissistic behavior, giving readers with the skills they need to protect themselves and move on in a healthy and good way. Whether or not you are looking to improve your relationships, strengthen your boundaries, or simply gain a deeper understanding of the narcissistic personality traits, "The Narcissist's Nightmare in

Sixty Minutes" is a priceless tool that will help you navigate the complex world of narcissism with confidence and clarity.

"……………….. my focus on this subject seeks to cast a spotlight predominantly on "Religious narcissism." Having grown and lived in Africa, for many years where religious fanaticism is prevalent, I have quite encountered practical and daunting experiences with religious narcissists. I have friends who have also suffered deep wounds from this behavioral plague. I have seen first-hand, church members being manipulated, abused and the extortion money and valuable items from them only for selfish gain. For some unknown reason, I had not crossed path with the intricacies surrounding the cliché "narcissism" until a couple of years down the line.

While in college, my desire to understand why these people were so entitled to themselves grew much wider, that was how I started seeking knowledge to solve the puzzles regarding this particular behavioral trait.

These people taught us to live our lives to please God, they taught us righteousness and how to metamorphose into fervent Christians, but guess what? they were narcissists.

It was close to impossible to express yourself when you think you are being treated wrong or explain how you feel about something you think isn't right or needed to be done the other way.

The biggest challenge was finding myself and letting go of all that I went through after coming to understanding that they themselves didn't know who they were.

The most detrimental part of narcissism is that; most narcissists probably wouldn't know they were narcissists until it's too late. Thus, the infestation with their narcissistic venom had already taken place and many have been left groping in the dark confinements of narcissistic tendencies......... "

CHAPTER 1

Who is a Narcissist?

A **narcissist** is a person who has an **excessive feeling of self-importance** as well as an **unquenchable yearning for adulation and attention**. Narcissism can take many forms and it is crucial to understand each one of them and the impact it can have on its victims.

The term "narcissism" is taken from the name of a Greek mythological figure: Narcissus, the son of a deity, who fell in love with his own reflection in the waters of a spring.

Holly Crisp-Han, MD, a psychiatrist and clinical associate professor at Baylor College of Medicine in Houston and the co-author of Narcissism and Its Discontents, believes everyone has narcissistic tendencies from time to time.

However, such traits become a personality disorder when a person's capacity to operate and connect with others is compromised. (Kritz, 2022)

This book Outlays all the vivid strategies to help deal with this type of behavior.

How narcissists are formed

According to Cleveland Clinic (n.d), experts believe that up to 5% of individuals have NPD. Narcissism is one of 10 personality disorders. These disorder leads individuals to think, feel and act in ways that damage themselves or others. Signs of personality problems commonly arise in the late teen years and early adulthood.

The formation of narcissists is a complex and multifaceted

process that can have a variety of underlying causes. While there is no single definitive answer to this question, some research suggests that narcissism may develop as a result of a combination of genetic, environmental, and social factors.

One theory according to Cleveland Clinic (n.d), is that some people may be born with a genetic predisposition to narcissism, meaning they may be more likely to develop the trait if certain environmental factors are present. For example, a study published in the Journal of Personality and Social Psychology found that individuals with a particular variant of the oxytocin receptor gene may be more susceptible to developing narcissistic traits when exposed to stress and social rejection.

In addition to genetic factors, environmental and social influences can also play a role in the development of narcissism. For example, some psychologists believe that children who are raised in environments where they are consistently praised and rewarded for their accomplishments, and where their needs are always prioritized, may be more likely to develop narcissistic traits. Similarly, children who are subjected to emotional abuse or neglect may also be at increased risk for developing narcissistic tendencies as a way of coping with feelings of inadequacy or insecurity.

Some scholars believe that cultural and socioeconomic influences might also impact narcissism. Individualism and self-promotion, for example, are highly prized in some cultures, and persons with narcissistic qualities may be more likely to be rewarded and commended for their conduct. Collectivism and humility may be more highly regarded in other cultures, whereas narcissistic tendencies may be seen poorly.

Parenting techniques can also play a role in the development of narcissism. Overly critical, demanding, or perfectionistic parents may foster an environment in which their children believe they will never measure up, leading to feelings of inadequacy and a drive to compensate for perceived inadequacies. Parents who are extremely indulgent or lenient, on the other hand, may create an environment in which their children feel entitled and unduly self-important.

It is also important to note that narcissism may emerge at various phases of life. Some people, for example, may develop narcissistic qualities as a result of a traumatic incident or big life transition, such as divorce or job loss. Similarly, some mental health disorders, such as borderline personality disorder, may be linked to the development of narcissistic personality disorder.

In conclusion, the development of narcissism is a

complicated and varied process that can be impacted by a multitude of factors, including genetics, environmental and cultural influences, parenting methods, and life experiences.

Overall, it is vital to recognize that the development of narcissism is a complicated and varied process that varies greatly from person to person. While there is no one "cause" of narcissism, recognizing the numerous elements that might contribute to its development may help individuals and mental health professionals recognize and treat the disorder more effectively. (Pederson, 2021)

1. IDEALIZE
The idealization stage is sometimes called the honeymoon stage is where the narcissist puts you on a pedestal. It's intoxicating, consuming, and exciting. The idealization stage has lots of feel-good vibes flowing. It's full of hope, and endless possibilities.

4. HOOVER
In the hoover stage, the narcissist tries to suck you back into their grasp. You will see a glimpse of the person you were once connected to in the very beginning. At this stage, the narcissist is attempting to start the narcissistic cycle of abuse all over again.

The Narcissistic Cycle of Abuse

2. DEVALUE
In the devaluation stage, the narcissist has lost interest in you. You are no longer the top priority of the narcissist. You have been dethroned and have lost your place of value to the narcissist. The narcissist's true character begins to show.

@flourishinghope.com

3. DISCARD
In the discard stage, the narcissist ends the connection with you. The narcissist no longer has a use for you, so they discard you. The narcissist may have found a new source of supply or target of interest. The discard may be abrupt, ghosting, or a gradual withdrawal.

CHAPTER 2

The Narcissist's Target

Narcissists tend to target individuals who they perceive as weaker or more vulnerable, as well as those who they believe will be more likely to provide them with the admiration, attention, and validation they crave. This can include romantic partners, family members, friends, coworkers, and even strangers.

One common target of narcissists is individuals with low self-esteem or those who have been through a traumatic experience, as they may be more susceptible to manipulation and less likely to resist the narcissist's attempts to control them. Narcissists may also target individuals who are highly empathetic, as they can use this empathy to their advantage in gaining sympathy and support from others.

Narcissists may also target individuals who they view as a

threat to their own sense of superiority or self-importance. For example, a narcissistic boss may target an employee who is seen as a potential rival, while a narcissistic partner may target a significant other who is seen as having qualities or accomplishments that could potentially outshine their own.

It is also worth noting that narcissists may target those who they believe are simple to manipulate or control. Individuals who are too trusting, emotionally sensitive, or who put others' needs ahead of their own might fall into this category.

They may also target those who they believe have something they desire or require, such as money, position, or connections. They may employ flattery, charm, and manipulation to acquire their targets' trust and admiration, and then exploit this to obtain access to their resources.

Narcissists may also attack people they perceive to be in positions of power or authority.

influence, since they may perceive these people as a means to their own ends. A narcissistic politician, for example, may target affluent contributors to garner financial support for their campaign, whereas a narcissistic employee may target their boss to gain promotions or other career progression chances.

Narcissists may target groups of people in addition to single individuals. They may utilize their charisma and charm, for example, to acquire the support and admiration of a certain social group or community, or they may use their position of power to influence and dominate a group of employees or colleagues.

Overall, narcissists' targets might be a wide range of people, but they are usually people that the narcissist sees as beneficial in achieving their own wants and ambitions, while also being prone to manipulation and control. It is crucial to highlight that being targeted by a narcissist does not represent the individual's worth or value, and getting help from a mental health professional or a trusted friend or family member can be an important step in breaking free from narcissistic control.

CHAPTER 3

The Biochemical Bonds That Get Us "Hooked"
On Narcissists

Narcissists may be incredibly attractive and charismatic, attracting people easily. The molecular relationships that keep us "hooked" on narcissists, on the other hand, might be more complicated than mere attraction. In this essay, we will look at some of the biological processes that take place when we get emotionally attracted to a narcissist.

The release of the neurotransmitter dopamine is the initial biological link that holds us to narcissists. Dopamine is the neurotransmitter responsible for the sensations of pleasure and reward, and it is released in reaction to pleasant events such as falling in love. while we grow attracted to a narcissist, the brain responds by releasing dopamine in reaction to the pleasurable sensations we experience while we are in their presence.

The release of oxytocin is another biological tie that keeps us attracted to narcissists. Oxytocin, sometimes known as the "cuddle hormone," is a hormone that is released in reaction to physical contact and emotional attachment. When we become emotionally and physically engaged to a narcissist, our brains release oxytocin in reaction to the physical and emotional connection we feel. This produces a sensation of closeness and intimacy that is tough to let go of.

The release of cortisol is the third biological tie that keeps us attracted to narcissists. Cortisol is a hormone that is secreted in reaction to stress and is commonly known as the "stress hormone." When we grow emotionally engaged to a narcissist, our brains release cortisol in reaction to the stress and anxiety we experience in the relationship. This creates a sense of addiction, as the brain begins to associate the release of cortisol with the presence of the narcissist.

In conclusion, the biochemical bonds that keep us "hooked" on narcissists are complex and multi-faceted. The release of dopamine, oxytocin, and cortisol creates a potent combination of pleasure, intimacy, and addiction that can be difficult to resist.

CHAPTER 4

Narcissistic abuse is a type of emotional and psychological manipulation perpetrated by people who have a narcissistic personality disorder. It can manifest itself in a variety of ways, leaving the victim feeling befuddled, alienated, and emotionally depleted. Here are several indicators that you may have been abused by a narcissist:

- You constantly feel on edge: Narcissistic abusers often use gas lighting techniques, which make you question your own perception of reality. You may start to doubt your own memories, feelings, and even sanity. This can lead to feeling constantly anxious and on edge.

- You feel isolated from friends and family:

Narcissistic abusers often try to isolate their victims from their support network. They may discourage you from seeing your friends and family or even turn them against you by spreading lies and rumors.

- You feel like you're walking on eggshells: Narcissistic abusers can be unpredictable and volatile. You may feel like you're constantly walking on eggshells around them, afraid to say or do anything that may upset them.

- You feel like you're always wrong: Narcissistic abusers often have a need to be right and may belittle or criticize you for your opinions, ideas, or actions. You may start to feel like you're always wrong and that nothing you do is good enough.

- You have a low sense of self-worth: Narcissistic abusers often manipulate their victims into feeling like they're not good enough. They may make you feel like you're the problem and that everything that goes wrong in the relationship is your fault. This can lead to feelings of low self-worth and self-doubt.

- You feel like you're constantly giving and not receiving: Narcissistic abusers often take advantage of their victims by using them for their own needs and desires. You may feel like you're constantly giving and not receiving anything in return.

- You feel like you're losing yourself: Narcissistic abusers can be very controlling and may try to mold you into their ideal image of you. You may start to lose your sense of self and feel like you're living someone else's life.

Childhood Programming that makes you a Magnet for Narcissists

Childhood programming that attracts narcissists is frequently founded in early experiences of neglect, emotional abuse, or trauma. Children who do not get continuous affection, attention, and affirmation as they grow up are more prone to develop a strong feeling of insecurity and poor self-worth. This makes individuals prone to narcissists' manipulative techniques, since they are good at exploiting others' weaknesses to acquire power and control.

Emotional neglect is a prevalent kind of early programming that renders people more vulnerable to narcissistic abuse. Emotional neglect happens when a kid's emotional needs are unmet, either because caregivers are emotionally unavailable or because the child is emotionally unavailable and actively discouraged from expressing their feelings. Children who grow up in emotionally neglectful environments may develop a deep-seated fear of abandonment and rejection, as well as a sense of shame and self-doubt. These feelings can make them vulnerable to the intense charm and flattery of narcissists, who often use love-bombing and other manipulative tactics to gain the trust and admiration of their targets.

Another form of childhood programming that can make individuals more susceptible to narcissistic abuse is emotional abuse. Emotional abuse can take many forms, including gaslighting, criticism, humiliation, and belittlement. Children who grow up in emotionally abusive environments may develop a distorted sense of self-worth, as well as a tendency to doubt their own perceptions and feelings. This can expose individuals to narcissists' gaslighting methods, which frequently aim to undermine their victims' sense of reality and control.

Finally, early trauma such as physical or sexual abuse might predispose people to narcissistic abuse. Trauma can result in a variety of emotional and psychological problems, such as PTSD, anxiety, despair, and substance misuse. Individuals who have endured childhood trauma may develop emotions of shame, remorse, and self-doubt, making them open to narcissists' manipulative techniques.

Healing from childhood brainwashing that has made you a narcissistic magnet may be a difficult but ultimately rewarding process. Here are some ways to begin the healing process:

1. **Recognize the patterns**: Start by recognizing the patterns in your life that make you vulnerable to narcissistic abuse. For example, you may have a pattern of putting others' needs before your own or accepting blame for things that are not your fault.

2. Identify the source of the programming: Once you recognize the patterns, try to identify where they come from. It could be from your childhood experiences, such as having a narcissistic parent or caregiver. Understanding the source can help you to heal more effectively.

3. **Challenge negative beliefs:** Childhood programming often includes negative beliefs about yourself, such as "I'm not good enough" or "I don't deserve love." Challenge these beliefs by recognizing that they are not true and focusing on

positive affirmations instead.

4. **Practice self-care:** Practicing self-care can help you to develop a stronger sense of self and reduce your vulnerability to narcissistic abuse. This can include things like exercise, meditation, therapy, and spending time with supportive friends and family members.

5. **Set healthy boundaries**: Setting healthy boundaries is essential when it comes to avoiding narcissistic abuse. Learn to say "no" to things that do not serve you, and surround yourself with people who respect your boundaries.

6. **Seek professional help:** Healing childhood programming can be challenging, and it may be helpful to seek the guidance of a therapist or counselor who can provide support and guidance as

you work through the process.

Remember that healing takes time and patience, but it is worth the effort to break free from the cycle of narcissistic abuse and develop healthy, loving relationships.

CHAPTER 5

Narcissists can be found in all walks of life, and in a variety of settings. They may be found in the workplace, in social circles, in families, and even in romantic relationships. Some common places where narcissists can be found include:

- **The workplace**: Narcissists may be drawn to positions of power and authority, such as management or executive roles, where they can assert their dominance and control over others.

- **Social media**: Social media platforms can provide an ideal platform for narcissists to showcase their accomplishments and seek attention and validation.

- **Romantic relationships**: Narcissists may seek out partners who can boost their self-esteem and make them feel superior, and may engage in manipulative behaviors such as love bombing to gain control over their partners.

- **Family:** Narcissists may exhibit their narcissistic tendencies within their family dynamics, and may seek to control and manipulate family members for their own benefit.

- **Religion:** Narcissists can also be found in religious settings, just like any other setting. In fact, some studies have suggested that religious leaders and clergy members may be particularly susceptible to developing narcissistic traits, due to the authority and power that comes with their positions.

- **Political systems:** Narcissists in political systems are not uncommon and can have a significant impact on the functioning of the political system. It's important to recognize the potential impact of narcissistic politicians on the political system and to hold them accountable for their actions.

The workplace Narcissist

The workplace is a popular location for numerous types of abuse, including but not limited to narcissistic abuse. Here are some symptoms that you may be subjected to narcissistic workplace abuse:

- Your boss or coworker frequently belittles or criticizes you: Narcissistic abusers may use their power or authority in the workplace to put others down and make them feel inferior. They may belittle or criticize your work or ideas, making you feel like you're never good enough.

- You feel like you're walking on eggshells around your boss or coworker: Narcissistic abusers can be unpredictable and volatile. You may feel like you're constantly walking on eggshells around them, afraid to say or do anything that may upset them.

- Your boss or coworker takes credit for your work: Narcissistic abusers may try to take credit for your successes or ideas in the workplace. They may also blame you for their mistakes or shortcomings, even if you had nothing to do with it.

- You're constantly being monitored or micromanaged: Narcissistic abusers may try to control every aspect of your work, from your schedule to your methods. They may constantly monitor your progress or demand updates on your work, making you feel like you're not trusted.

- You feel isolated from your coworkers or team: Narcissistic abusers may try to isolate you from your coworkers or team, either by creating conflicts or by undermining your relationships with others. This can make you feel alone and unsupported in the workplace.

- You're expected to cater to your boss or coworker's every need: Narcissistic abusers may demand that you prioritize their needs over your own, even if it's not necessary or reasonable. They may also try to guilt-trip or manipulate you into doing things for them.

- You feel like you're constantly trying to prove yourself: Narcissistic abusers may make you feel like you're never good enough and that you need to constantly prove yourself to them. This can lead to feelings of anxiety, stress, and burnout.

The religious Narcissists.

Religious narcissism is a phenomenon in which narcissistic people use religion to boost their own self-image and acquire power and control over others. This can present itself in a variety of ways, including abusing their positions of power within religious groups, using religious beliefs to excuse their own self-serving conduct, and seeking adoration and attention from their followers or congregation.

Religious narcissism, at its root, entails utilizing religion to satisfy one's personal wants and goals, rather than serving a higher force or aiding others. Narcissistic people may regard their religious views or practices as superior to those of others, and they may perceive their religious group as a source of adulation and validation.

For the above avenues that the narcissist operates, my interest has been biased towards Religious narcissism. Having grown and lived in Africa, for many years where religious fanaticism is prevalent, I have quite encountered practical and daunting experiences with religious narcissists. I have friends who have also suffered deep wounds from this behavioral plague. I have seen first-hand, members being manipulated to extort money and valuable items from them for their own selfish gain. For lack of knowledge, I didn't know anything about narcissism until a couple of years down the line and the eye opening all begun.

While in college, my desire to understand why these people were so entitled to themselves grew much wider, that was how come I started seeking knowledge to solve the puzzles regarding this particular behavior.

At some point in time, I experienced some extent of

narcissistic abuse and it was from the local church I was fellowshipping with. Well, yours may not be from a Christian setting but yes, you sure might have experienced it from an Islamic, Buddhist or any other religious setting you can mention.

These people taught us to live our lives to please God, they taught us righteousness and how to metamorphose into fervent Christians, but guess what? they were narcissists. And If you ask me I can tell you.

It was close to impossible to express yourself when you think you are being treated wrong or explain how you feel about something you think isn't right or needs to be done the other way. Come on now! Oh I forgot, you dare not confront them when they embarrass you in front of the whole congregation, no you dare not because you are going to be the most disrespectful person the Church has ever known. Another problem that paved the way for this was the fact that, I didn't really know who I was and this is the same reason many people go through narcissistic abuse.

This is just to mention but a few, the biggest challenge was finding myself and letting go of all that I went through after understanding that they themselves didn't know who they were. The most detrimental part of narcissism is that; most narcissists probably wouldn't know they were narcissists until it's too late. Thus, the infestation with their narcissistic venom had already taken place and many have been left groping in the dark confinements of narcissistic tendencies.

Some common behaviors associated with religious narcissism include:

- **Exploiting positions of authority**: Narcissistic individuals may seek out positions of authority within religious organizations, such as leadership roles or positions of influence. They may use their authority to control and manipulate others, and to further their own goals and desires.

- **Using religious teachings to justify self-serving behaviors**: Religious narcissists may twist or manipulate religious teachings to justify their own self-serving behaviors. For example, they may use religious texts to justify their own greed or desire for power.

- **Belittling or dismissing the beliefs and opinions of others:** Narcissistic individuals may see their own beliefs and opinions as superior to those of others, and may belittle or dismiss the beliefs and opinions of others within their religious community.

- **Seeking admiration and attention**: Religious narcissists may use their religious community as a means of gaining admiration and attention from others. They may seek to be seen as a spiritual authority or guru, and may use their charisma and charm to gain followers.

Romantic relationships

Narcissistic behavior can also show up in romantic relationships, and it can have a damaging impact on the partner who is on the receiving end of it. Here are some signs that you may be in a relationship with a narcissist:

- **Grandiose sense of self**: Narcissists often have an inflated sense of self-importance and may believe that they are superior to others. They may talk about themselves a lot and show little interest in your life or feelings.

- **Lack of empathy:** Narcissists may struggle to empathize with their partner's feelings or experiences. They may dismiss your concerns or be insensitive to your emotions.

- **Need for admiration**: Narcissists may constantly seek admiration and praise from their partner. They may fish for compliments or become upset if they feel like they are not receiving enough attention.

- **Manipulative behavior**: Narcissists may use manipulation tactics to get what they want in the relationship. They may guilt-trip, gaslight, or lie to their partner to maintain control.

- **Jealousy and possessiveness**: Narcissists may become jealous and possessive of their partner, even if there is no reason for it. They may accuse their partner of cheating or be overly controlling of their actions and behaviors.

- **Lack of boundaries**: Narcissists may have little regard for their partner's boundaries and may push them to do things they are not comfortable with. They may also be insensitive to their partner's need for personal space or privacy.

- **Emotional volatility**: Narcissists may have intense emotional reactions to minor incidents, becoming angry or upset over small things. This can create a tense and unpredictable atmosphere in the relationship.

Family

Narcissistic behavior can also occur within families and can be particularly damaging to the emotional well-being of family members. Here are some signs that you may be dealing with a narcissistic family member:

- Self-centeredness: Narcissistic family members often put their own needs and desires ahead of others. They may dominate conversations, ignore the feelings and experiences of others, and demand attention and admiration.

- **Lack of empathy**: Narcissists may struggle to understand or show empathy towards the feelings and experiences of their family members. They may dismiss their concerns or be insensitive to their emotional needs.

- **Blame-shifting:** Narcissists may blame others for their problems and shortcomings, refusing to take responsibility for their actions. They may also project their own flaws onto others, making their family members feel responsible for their negative behaviors.

- **Manipulation**: Narcissists may use manipulation tactics to control their family members. They may guilt-trip, gaslight, or threaten to cut off their family members to get what they want.

- Envy and competition: Narcissistic family members

may be envious of the accomplishments or successes of their family members and may engage in competitive behaviors to maintain their own sense of superiority.

- Disrespect for boundaries: Narcissistic family members may have little respect for the boundaries of their family members, including their need for personal space, privacy, or autonomy.

Political Narcissists

Manipulation and deceit are common tactics used by narcissistic politicians to achieve their goals and maintain their power. Here are some ways they may engage in manipulation and deceit:

1. **Grandiose promises:** Narcissistic politicians may make extravagant promises and unrealistic claims to appeal to voters. They may promise to solve complex problems quickly or offer easy solutions to complex issues without providing concrete plans or details.

2. **Distorting the truth**: Narcissistic politicians may twist facts or distort the truth to suit their agenda or image. They may use selective information or half-truths to manipulate public opinion and create a favorable narrative.

3. **Propaganda**: Narcissistic politicians may use propaganda to control public opinion and maintain their image. They may use biased media outlets or social media platforms to disseminate their message and suppress opposing viewpoints.

4. **Gaslighting:** Narcissistic politicians may engage in

gas lighting, a manipulative tactic that involves making someone doubt their own perception of reality. They may deny or dismiss facts, rewrite history, or blame others for their failures.

5. Scapegoating: Narcissistic politicians may scapegoat certain groups or individuals to deflect blame and create a common enemy. They may use fear-mongering and demonization to create a sense of urgency or rally support behind their cause.

Dealing with a narcissistic politician can be challenging, but it's important to stay informed and engaged in the political process. It's essential to fact-check information and seek out diverse perspectives to avoid falling prey to propaganda or manipulation. Maintaining a healthy skepticism and holding politicians accountable for their actions and words can help promote transparency and honesty in politics. Additionally, supporting independent media outlets and grassroots organizations can help challenge the dominant narratives and give voice to underrepresented communities.

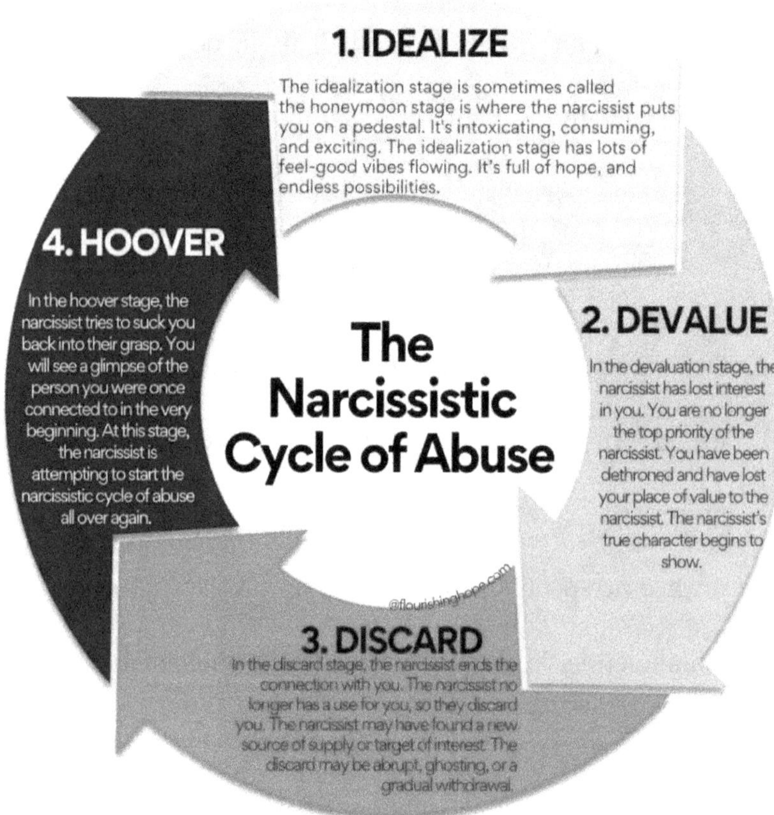

Signs of Narcissistic Abuse

1. Love bombing followed by devaluation. Intense praise followed by verbal abuse.

2. Gaslighting: making you disbelieve reality or feel like you're losing your grasp on reality.

3. Intentionally sabotaging friendships or other relationships.

4. Making you the enemy or bad guy for having feelings and reactions.

5. Constant lying to avoid responsibility.

6. Never being at fault for any issues in the relationship. Turning all of the blame toward you.

7. Having a lack of interest in who you are as a person.

8. A huge sense of entitlement. You owe them everything.

Read more on BlessingManifesting

CHAPTER 6

Types of Narcissists

Narcissism is a personality disorder marked by a grandiose feeling of self-importance, an obsession with dreams of endless prosperity, power, intelligence, beauty, or perfect love, and a lack of empathy for others. There are various sorts of narcissists, each with its own set of characteristics and actions. Here are some of the most prevalent types:

A grandiose narcissist

A grandiose narcissist is a type of person who has an inflated sense of self-importance and believes they are superior to others. They often have an exaggerated sense of their own achievements and talents, and they expect admiration and special treatment from others. They may come across as arrogant, entitled, and boastful, and may have a tendency to belittle or demean those they consider inferior to themselves.

Grandiose narcissists tend to be highly confident and assertive, and they may be drawn to positions of power or influence where they can exercise control over others. They may have a charismatic personality that attracts others to them, but their relationships are often characterized by a lack of empathy and a tendency to exploit others for their own gain.

Despite their outward confidence, grandiose narcissists may be deeply insecure and vulnerable to criticism or rejection. They may become defensive or aggressive when their sense of self-worth is challenged, and may lash out at those who they perceive as threatening to their ego.

In relationships, grandiose narcissists may struggle to form deep connections with others. They may view others as objects to be used for their own purposes, rather than as individuals with their own thoughts, feelings, and needs.

They may also struggle with intimacy, as they may fear vulnerability and perceive emotional closeness as a threat to their sense of control.

Regardless of their weaknesses, grandiose narcissists may be adept at attaining their objectives and may have a track record of success in their employment or personal life. They may be charming and influential, inspiring others to follow their lead. Their actions, however, may eventually come back to haunt them, as their lack of empathy and disrespect for others may lead them to lose the support and trust of people around them.

It's crucial to remember that grandiose narcissism is a personality trait that occurs on a spectrum, and not everyone with narcissistic features is a full-fledged narcissist.

Furthermore, while grandiose narcissism may be destructive to individuals and society as a whole, it's vital to understand that people with this trait can have excellent traits and can change with the correct assistance and tools.

Overall, a grandiose narcissist is someone who believes they are exceptional, deserve special attention, and wants others to recognize and affirm their superiority. Grandiose narcissists frequently have a sense of entitlement, believing that they are above the norms that apply to others. They may engage in unethical or even unlawful activities, and they may justify these actions by persuading themselves that they are legitimate because of their higher standing.

Vulnerable Narcissist

A vulnerable narcissist is someone who has low self-esteem and is easily wounded or offended. They may look timid or introverted, yet they are extremely sensitive to criticism and rejection. They may feel inferior or inadequate on the inside, yet they try hard to present a favorable picture to others.

Despite their self-doubt, vulnerable narcissists may have a strong desire for attention and recognition. They may seek validation from others and become upset or even enraged if they feel that their needs are not being met. They may have a tendency to blame others for their problems and may struggle to take responsibility for their actions.

In relationships, vulnerable narcissists may be needy and demanding. They may expect their partners to cater to their every whim and may become angry or resentful if their needs are not met. They may also have difficulty with intimacy, as they may fear being rejected or abandoned by those they care about.

Vulnerable narcissists may also struggle with jealousy and envy. They may become fixated on others who they perceive as more successful or attractive than themselves and may feel a deep sense of inferiority as a result. They may also engage in gossip or negative talk about others in order to elevate themselves in the eyes of others.

They may have positive attributes in addition to their bad traits. They may be empathic and compassionate to others, and they may be able to develop profound bonds with individuals in whom they have faith. Vulnerable narcissists may be able to overcome their fears and build a stronger sense of self-esteem with the correct assistance and tools. Vulnerable narcissists may also struggle with self-regulation and have a proclivity to engage in harmful behaviors impulsive or self-destructive behaviors. They may turn to drugs, alcohol, or other unhealthy coping mechanisms in order to escape their negative feelings or to seek temporary relief from their emotional pain.

In addition, vulnerable narcissists may be prone to depression and anxiety. They may struggle with feelings of hopelessness and despair, and may have difficulty finding joy or meaning in their lives. They may also be highly sensitive to stress and may struggle to cope with change or uncertainty.

Vulnerable narcissists may be able to accomplish personal development and transformation with the correct assistance and tools. Therapy can be especially beneficial for vulnerable narcissists because it provides a secure and supportive setting in which to analyze their feelings, beliefs, and actions. Vulnerable narcissists may start to construct a more meaningful and happy existence by learning healthy coping mechanisms, building a more realistic sense of self, and nurturing more positive interactions.

There are several varieties of susceptible narcissists, each with its own set of qualities and inclinations. Below are a few instances:

The inverted narcissist

Inverted narcissism is a subtype of vulnerable narcissist who appears to lack self-esteem and may even put themselves down in front of others, but deep down they crave attention and validation. The term "inverted" refers to the fact that this type of narcissist has a self-concept that is the opposite of what we typically associate with narcissism.

Inverted narcissists may struggle with a deep sense of shame or inferiority, and they may seek to avoid the spotlight or attention from others as a way to protect themselves from rejection or criticism. They may appear shy, introverted, or withdrawn, but they are highly attuned to others' opinions of them and may become distressed if they feel they are not receiving the attention or validation they crave.

Despite their apparent lack of self-esteem, inverted narcissists may be highly skilled at manipulating others to meet their emotional needs. They may rely heavily on others for emotional support and may become overly attached to those who they perceive as being able to provide them with the attention they crave. They may use self-deprecating humor or play the role of a helpless victim in order to gain sympathy or attention from others.

Inverted narcissists may also struggle with feelings of envy or jealousy towards others who they perceive as more successful or attractive than themselves. They may harbor deep-seated feelings of inadequacy or inferiority, and may become overly focused on their perceived shortcomings.

Hypersensitive Narcissist

A hypersensitive narcissist is a subtype of vulnerable narcissist who is easily offended and may react strongly to perceived criticism or rejection. They may be highly attuned to others' opinions of them and may be quick to defend themselves or become defensive when they feel their self-worth is being challenged.

Hypersensitive narcissists may have a fragile sense of self-esteem and may rely heavily on others for validation and support. They may have a deep-seated fear of rejection or abandonment and may go to great lengths to avoid situations that could trigger these feelings.

Hypersensitive narcissists may be too reactive to stress and have difficulty dealing with unpleasant emotions. When they do not receive the attention or affirmation they seek, they may lash out at others or become angry or resentful.

The victim Narcissist

This is also a sub-category of vulnerable narcissist who portrays themselves as a victim of circumstances or of other people's mistreatment. They may blame others for their problems and may use their perceived victimhood as a way to gain sympathy and attention from others. They may also use guilt and manipulation to get others to do what they want.

Victim narcissists may have a deep-seated belief that they are entitled to special treatment or that the world owes them something. They may feel that they have been unfairly treated by others and may seek to gain power or control through their victim status.

Victim narcissists may be highly skilled at manipulating others to meet their emotional needs. They may use guilt, pity, or other tactics to get others to do what they want, or to make others feel sorry for them.

Victim narcissists may also struggle with feelings of envy or jealousy towards others who they perceive as having more power or success than themselves. They may harbor deep-seated feelings of inadequacy or inferiority, and may become overly focused on their perceived shortcomings.

Covert narcissist

Covert narcissism is a type of narcissist who displays many of the same traits as a standard or overt narcissist, but in a subtler and less obvious way. They may come across as shy, introverted, or self-effacing, but underneath this facade, they have a grandiose sense of self and a deep need for admiration and attention.

Unlike overt narcissists who are often loud and boastful about their accomplishments, covert narcissists may downplay their achievements and seek out praise and recognition in subtler ways. They may also use passive-aggressive tactics to control and manipulate others, such as guilt-tripping, playing the victim, or giving the silent treatment.

Covert narcissists may also struggle with feelings of insecurity and low self-esteem, which can manifest in behaviors such as excessive jealousy, possessiveness, or controlling behavior. They may also be highly sensitive to criticism or rejection and may react with anger or defensiveness.

Overall, while the behavior of a covert narcissist may not be as obvious as that of an overt narcissist, they can still be highly destructive and damaging to those around them

may also exhibit behaviors such as gas lighting, which is a tactic used to manipulate others by making them doubt their own perception of reality. They may also engage in emotional blackmail, using threats or emotional appeals to get what they want.

One of the key features of a covert narcissist is their ability to project a false image of themselves as kind, caring, and empathetic individuals, even though they lack genuine empathy for others. They may use this image to manipulate and control others, while simultaneously avoiding criticism or blame.

In relationships, covert narcissists may be emotionally distant, controlling, and manipulative. They may struggle with intimacy and may be prone to cheating or engaging in other forms of infidelity. They may also be highly sensitive to rejection or abandonment and may react with anger or resentment if they feel that their partner is not meeting their needs.

While covert narcissists may appear to be less destructive than overt narcissists, they can still cause significant harm to those around them. It is important to be aware of the signs of covert narcissism and to seek help if you or someone you know is struggling with this condition.

A Communal narcissist

A communal narcissist is a type of narcissist who seeks admiration and attention by presenting themselves as selfless and altruistic. They believe that they are superior to others because they are more giving, compassionate, and empathetic than the average person.

Communal narcissists may engage in charitable or humanitarian work, and they may be very active in their community or religious group. They may also present themselves as humble and self-effacing, downplaying their own achievements and emphasizing the needs of others.

However, beneath this façade of selflessness, communal narcissists still have a deep need for admiration and attention. They may become resentful or angry if they feel that their efforts are not appreciated or if others do not recognize their contributions.

In relationships, communal narcissists may use their altruistic behavior as a way to control and manipulate others. They may use guilt or obligation to get their partners to do what they want, or they may become angry or resentful if their partner does not appreciate their selflessness.

One of the key features of communal narcissism is the belief that they are superior to others because of their ability to give and care for others. They may view themselves as more morally superior or spiritually advanced than others, and may feel entitled to recognition and praise for their efforts.

Communal narcissists may also struggle with feelings of emptiness or worthlessness, which they may try to fill by seeking admiration and attention through their selfless acts. However, their need for validation can never truly be satisfied, which may lead them to become increasingly demanding or manipulative in their behavior.

In some cases, communal narcissists may also use their altruistic behavior as a way to avoid dealing with their own emotional issues or personal problems. They may project their own insecurities onto others, or use their giving behavior as a way to avoid taking responsibility for their own actions.

In conclusion, communal narcissism is a type of narcissism that is characterized by a need for admiration and attention through selfless acts. While they may present themselves as caring and compassionate individuals, their behavior is ultimately driven by a need for validation and recognition. It is important to be aware of the signs of communal narcissism and to seek help if you or someone you know is struggling with this condition

The Somatic narcissist

Somatic narcissists primarily focus on their physical appearance, sexual prowess, and attractiveness. They believe that their physical appearance and sexual abilities are superior to those of others, and they use this belief to gain admiration, attention, and validation from others.

Somatic narcissists may spend an excessive amount of time and money on their physical appearance, including clothing, grooming, cosmetic surgery, and fitness routines. They may also engage in sexual behaviors to gain attention and validation from others, and may view their sexual partners as objects to be used for their own pleasure and satisfaction.

One of the key characteristics of somatic narcissism is a lack of empathy for others. Somatic narcissists may be preoccupied with their own physical appearance and sexual desires to the extent that they disregard the feelings and needs of others. They may be quick to discard or devalue romantic partners who no longer meet their physical standards or sexual desires.

Somatic narcissists may also be prone to jealousy and competition, particularly when it comes to their physical appearance or sexual conquests. They may view others as rivals or threats to their own sense of superiority, and may engage in aggressive or manipulative behaviors to maintain their position of power.

Overall, somatic narcissism is a type of narcissism that is characterized by a preoccupation with physical appearance, sexual prowess, and attractiveness. While they may initially appear charming and attractive, somatic narcissists can be highly destructive and damaging to those around them, particularly in romantic relationships. Somatic narcissists may also have a sense of entitlement when it comes to their physical appearance and sexual attractiveness. They may believe that they are entitled to attention and admiration simply because of their physical beauty or sexual prowess, and may become angry or resentful if they feel that they are not getting the attention they believe they deserve.

In addition to their preoccupation with their own physical appearance and sexual abilities, somatic narcissists may also use their attractiveness as a way to manipulate and control others. They may use their charm and good looks to get what they want from others, and may be quick to discard or devalue those who no longer serve their purposes.

Somatic narcissists may also struggle with feelings of insecurity and inadequacy, which they may try to mask through their preoccupation with physical appearance and sexual prowess. They may view others as objects to be conquered or controlled, rather than as human beings with their own thoughts, feelings, and desires.

In relationships, somatic narcissists may be highly seductive and charming initially, but may become increasingly demanding and manipulative as the relationship progresses. They may become jealous or possessive of their partners, and may use their sexual abilities as a way to control and dominate them.

Somatic narcissism can be highly destructive and damaging to those around the individual. It is important to be aware of the signs of somatic narcissism and to seek help if you or someone you know is struggling with this condition. Treatment may involve therapy, medication, and other interventions to help the individual develop healthier ways of relating to others and managing their own self-esteem and self-worth.

The Cerebral Narcissist

A cerebral narcissist is a type of narcissist who is primarily focused on their intellectual abilities and achievements. They believe that they are intellectually superior to others and may view themselves as geniuses or prodigies. They use their intellectual abilities to gain admiration, attention, and validation from others.

Cerebral narcissists may be highly knowledgeable in a specific field, and may seek to use their expertise to dominate conversations and impress others. They may also engage in intellectual pursuits, such as reading, writing, or academic research, as a way to further validate their sense of superiority.

One of the key characteristics of cerebral narcissism is a lack of empathy for others. Cerebral narcissists may be so preoccupied with their own intellectual abilities and achievements that they disregard the thoughts, feelings, and needs of others. They may see others as inferior and may have little interest in developing relationships or connections with others.

Cerebral narcissists may also be prone to grandiosity and entitlement. They may believe that their intellectual abilities make them entitled to special treatment or privileges, and may become angry or resentful if they feel that they are not getting the attention or recognition they believe they deserve.

When in relationships, cerebral narcissists may be highly critical and demanding of their partners. They may view their partners as intellectual inferiors, and may become frustrated or dismissive if their partner does not share their interests or level of intelligence.

Cerebral narcissists may also use their intellectual abilities as a way to manipulate and control others. They may use their knowledge and expertise to convince others to follow their lead or to believe in their ideas, and may become angry or dismissive if others challenge their beliefs or opinions. They may also engage in intellectual one-upmanship, where they constantly seek to prove their intellectual superiority over others.

They may also struggle with feelings of inadequacy and insecurity, which they may try to mask through their preoccupation with intellectual pursuits and achievements. They may view their intellectual abilities as the only way to gain validation and self-worth, and may become obsessed with achieving more and more in their intellectual pursuits.

Cerebral narcissists may demonstrate perfectionism and rigidity in their thinking, in addition to a lack of empathy and grandiosity. They may have a strong desire for control and may get quite worried or irritated if things do not go as planned or as expected.

In relationships, cerebral narcissists may fail to connect emotionally with others. They may regard emotions as inferior to intellect and have no interest in forming emotional bonds with others. If their spouse displays feelings or needs that they do not understand or connect to, they may get annoyed or dismissive.

Cerebral narcissism is a type of narcissism that is characterized by a preoccupation with intellectual abilities and achievements. While they may initially appear intelligent and knowledgeable, cerebral narcissists can be highly destructive and damaging to those around them, particularly in personal relationships. It is important to be aware of the signs of cerebral narcissism and to seek help if you or someone you know is struggling with this condition. Treatment may involve therapy, medication, and other interventions to help the individual develop healthier ways of relating to others and managing their own self-esteem and self-worth.

It's worth noting that not all narcissists fit neatly into these categories, and some may exhibit traits from multiple types. Additionally, narcissism exists on a spectrum, and individuals may exhibit varying degrees of narcissistic behavior.

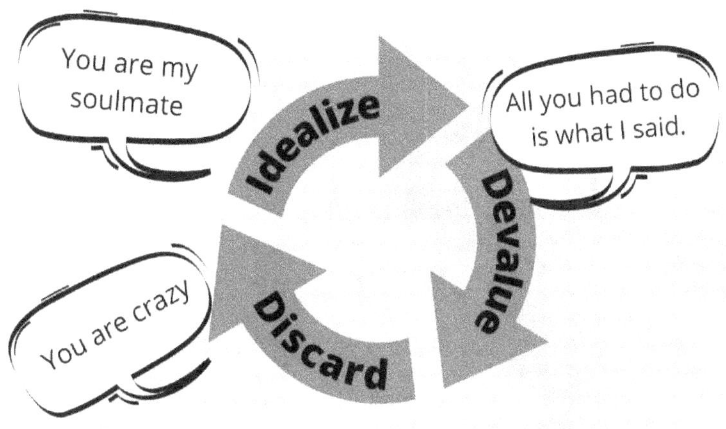
You are my soulmate
All you had to do is what I said.
You are crazy
Idealize
Devalue
Discard

CHAPTER 7

Victims' Emotional and Psychological Reasons for Staying in Narcissistic Abuse

Victims of narcissistic abuse are frequently locked in toxic relationships, despite the negative consequences for their emotional and psychological well-being. Victims may opt to remain in narcissistic abuse for a variety of emotional and psychological reasons. It is critical to understand these causes in order to give empathy and assistance to individuals in similar situations. *Here are some emotional and psychological reasons that lead to victims' continued involvement in narcissistic abuse.*

Fear of Repercussions: Narcissistic abusers frequently utilize a variety of techniques to engender terror in their victims. This anxiety might be physical, mental, or pecuniary in nature. Victims may fear vengeance, danger to themselves or loved ones, or reputational ruin. They may feel stuck and unwilling to leave the abusive relationship because they are afraid of the potential repercussions.

Belief in False Promises: Narcissistic abusers are skillful manipulators who may entice their victims back into the relationship by promising changes or improvements. They may apologize, express regret, or do brief acts of compassion, giving the victim hope that things will improve. Despite the pattern of abuse, the victim remains committed in the relationship because of the expectation for good change.

Emotional Dependency: Narcissistic abusers frequently

deceive their victims into being emotionally dependent on them. They may use methods like as love bombing, in which they lavish kindness and attention on their victims in order to build a deep emotional relationship. Victims may find it difficult to distance themselves from the abuser because they are afraid of losing the perceived emotional support and connection on which they have learned to rely.

Trauma Bonding: Trauma often displayed by narcissistic abuse can result in a one-of-a-kind link between the victim and the abuser, which is known as trauma bonding. This relationship forms as a result of the abuser's intermittent reinforcement of good and bad behavior. Victims may develop a psychological attachment to the abuser in the hope of recreating pleasant experiences and changing the abusive dynamics.

Financial Dependence: Victims may be financially reliant on the narcissistic abuser in some situations. This reliance might result from a lack of job, financial control, or economic manipulation. Victims who lack the resources to sustain themselves may feel imprisoned and unable to escape an abusive relationship.

CHAPTER 8

The Antidote

Narcissistic abuse is a form of emotional and psychological manipulation that can leave victims feeling depleted, isolated, and powerless. While there is no one-size-fits-all solution for healing from narcissistic abuse, there are some key strategies that can help victims to reclaim their power and rebuild their sense of self-worth. In this essay, we will explore some of the most effective antidotes to narcissistic abuse.

Firstly, it is important to recognize that healing from narcissistic abuse is a process that takes time, patience, and self-compassion. It is normal to feel overwhelmed and uncertain about where to begin, but the first step is to acknowledge that the abuse was not your fault and that you deserve to heal and move forward.

Setting boundaries

Narcissists tend to push boundaries and take advantage of people, so it's crucial to set clear limits on what you're willing to tolerate. Yes, setting boundaries is an essential step in dealing with narcissists. Narcissists often have a sense of entitlement and can take advantage of people, so setting clear limits on what you're willing to tolerate can help protect your well-being. It's important to communicate your boundaries assertively and stick to them, even if the narcissist tries to push back or violate them. This can help establish a sense of respect and autonomy in the relationship and prevent the narcissist from taking advantage of you.

In setting boundaries with narcissists, it's important to be specific and clear about what you're willing to tolerate and what you're not. This can include things like not accepting verbal abuse, not tolerating disrespect or manipulation, and setting limits on the amount of time you're willing to spend with the narcissist.

It's also important to enforce consequences if the narcissist violates your boundaries. For example, if the narcissist engages in a behavior that you've said you won't tolerate, it's important to follow through on the consequence you've outlined. This can help establish a sense of accountability in the relationship and make it clear that you won't tolerate being mistreated.

Additionally, it's important to set boundaries with empathy and compassion. Narcissists may not be aware of their behavior or may struggle with underlying mental health issues, and it's important to recognize this while also prioritizing your own well-being. By setting boundaries with empathy and kindness, you can maintain your own sense of integrity while also avoiding a power struggle or conflict with the narcissist.

It's also important to recognize when it's time to walk away from the relationship. If the narcissist consistently violates your boundaries, disrespects you, or makes you feel unsafe, it may be necessary to cut ties with them. This can be a difficult decision, but ultimately, your own well-being should be your top priority.

Another important aspect of setting boundaries with narcissists is practicing self-care. Dealing with narcissists can be emotionally draining, and it's important to prioritize your own well-being. This can include things like engaging in regular exercise, getting enough sleep, eating a healthy diet, and engaging in activities that bring you joy and fulfillment.

Don't engage in their drama

Narcissists thrive on attention, so don't engage in their drama or arguments. Stay calm and don't react emotionally. Yes, not engaging in a narcissist's drama is an important step in protecting your well-being. Narcissists thrive on attention and drama, and engaging with them can often escalate the situation and lead to more conflict. Instead, it's important to stay calm and not react emotionally to the narcissist's behavior.

One strategy for not engaging in the narcissist's drama is to focus on facts and logic rather than emotions. Narcissists often use emotional manipulation to get their way, and by staying focused on the facts of the situation, you can avoid getting drawn into their emotional games.

It's also important to practice mindfulness and self-awareness in dealing with narcissists. By being aware of your own emotions and reactions, you can better manage your responses to the narcissist's behavior and avoid getting caught up in their drama.

Remember, you can't control the narcissist's behavior, but you can control your own reactions. By staying calm and not engaging in their drama, you can protect your own well-being and maintain your sense of dignity and self-respect. Another way to avoid engaging in a narcissist's drama is to use "grey rock" technique. This means being unresponsive and emotionally neutral in your interactions with the narcissist. Avoid providing them with any emotional reactions or feedback, which can fuel their need for attention and drama. Instead, keep your responses short, factual, and unemotional.

It's also important to avoid getting caught up in the narcissist's games of manipulation and control. Narcissists often use tactics like gas lighting, projecting their own behavior onto others, and blaming others for their own actions. By recognizing these tactics and not getting drawn into them, you can maintain your sense of self-worth and avoid getting caught up in their drama.

In addition, it's important to prioritize your own needs and goals in dealing with narcissists. Don't let their drama and behavior distract you from your own priorities and values. Stay focused on your own well-being and goals, and don't let the narcissist's behavior derail you from achieving them.

Lastly, it's important to recognize that not engaging in the narcissist's drama may lead to them seeking attention elsewhere. They may try to provoke a reaction from others or find a new source of attention. Remember that you can't control their behavior, but you can control your own. By staying calm and not engaging in their drama, you can maintain your own sense of dignity and self-respect, regardless of how the narcissist chooses to behave.

Cut off their supply

Narcissists need a constant stream of admiration and attention, so don't give them what they want. Don't feed their ego or give them the validation they crave. Yes, not giving narcissists the attention and validation they crave is an important way to protect yourself from their manipulative behavior. Narcissists have an insatiable need for admiration, attention, and validation, which is often referred to as "narcissistic supply". By denying them this supply, you can weaken their hold on you and limit their ability to manipulate and control you.

One way to avoid giving narcissists supply is to avoid praising them excessively or giving them too much attention. Instead, focus on acknowledging their accomplishments or positive traits in a balanced and measured way. It's important to be sincere and genuine in your praise, but also to avoid inflating their ego or reinforcing their sense of entitlement.

Another way to avoid giving narcissists supply is to avoid engaging in their competitive games or power struggles. Narcissists often try to one-up others or assert their dominance in social situations. By refusing to engage in these games and instead focusing on your own goals and priorities, you can avoid giving them the attention and validation they crave.

It's also important to avoid being overly emotional or reactive in your interactions with narcissists. They may try to provoke a reaction from you to get the attention they need. By staying calm and non-reactive, you can avoid feeding their ego and maintain your own sense of emotional stability.

Remember, you have the power to control your own

behavior and reactions. By not giving narcissists the attention and validation they crave, you can protect yourself from their manipulative behavior and maintain your own sense of self-worth and dignity.

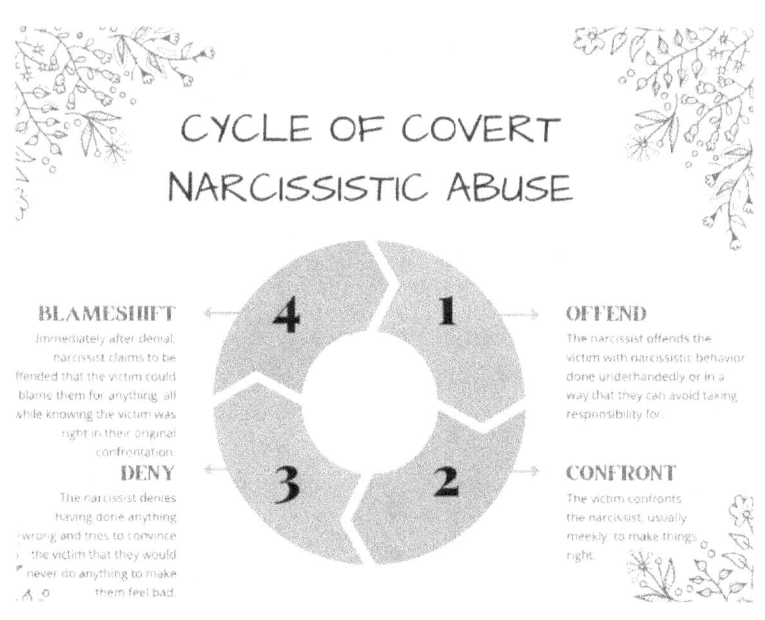

Stay independent

Narcissists like to control and manipulate people, so it's important to stay independent and not rely on them for anything. One way to do this is to set boundaries and assert your autonomy. Let them know that you are capable of making your own decisions and taking care of yourself. Be assertive, but also respectful and firm in your communication.

It may also be helpful to have a support system of friends and family who can provide emotional and practical support. Surrounding yourself with positive and supportive people can help you maintain your independence and resist the manipulative tactics of a narcissist.

Remember that you have the right to make choices that are in your best interest, and that it is not your responsibility to cater to the needs and demands of a narcissistic individual.

Don't let them gaslight you

Narcissists often manipulate and twist the truth to make themselves look good and others look bad. Don't let them gaslight you, and trust your own perceptions and feelings.

Yes, gaslighting is a common tactic used by narcissists to manipulate and control others. Gaslighting involves denying or distorting the truth in order to make the victim doubt their own perceptions and feelings. By recognizing when gaslighting is occurring and standing up for yourself, you can protect yourself from the narcissist's manipulation.

One way to avoid falling victim to gaslighting is to trust your own perceptions and feelings. Narcissists may try to make you doubt your own memories, perceptions, and experiences. By trusting your own gut instincts and seeking validation from trusted sources, such as friends or family members, you can maintain your own sense of reality.

It's also important to call out the narcissist's behavior when you recognize gaslighting occurring. This means standing up for yourself and refusing to accept their distorted version of reality. You can point out specific examples of the narcissist's behavior, express how it made you feel, and assert your own perspective.

Another way to protect yourself from gaslighting is to keep a record of events and interactions with the narcissist. This can help you to maintain your own sense of reality and provide evidence to support your own perspective. You can keep a journal, save messages or emails, or record conversations (if legal in your area) as evidence.

Remember, gaslighting is a form of emotional abuse and it is never acceptable. By recognizing the signs of gaslighting and standing up for yourself, you can protect yourself from the narcissist's manipulation and maintain your own sense of reality and self-worth.

Narcissists may try to manipulate your perceptions and feelings in a number of ways, such as by denying events or experiences, minimizing your feelings or experiences, or blaming you for their behavior.

If you recognize gaslighting occurring, it's important to respond in a calm and assertive manner. You can say something like, "I remember things differently" or "That's not how I remember it happening". It's also helpful to provide specific examples or evidence to support your own perspective.

It's important to remember that gaslighting is a form of emotional abuse and can have serious negative effects on your mental health and wellbeing. If you feel like you are experiencing gaslighting from a narcissist or anyone else, it may be helpful to seek professional support or talk to a trusted friend or family member.

Finally, it's important to remember that you have the power to set boundaries and make decisions that are in your own best interest. If the narcissist's behavior becomes abusive or intolerable, it may be necessary to cut ties or seek professional help. Remember that you deserve to be treated with respect and dignity, and you don't have to tolerate toxic or abusive behavior from anyone.

Educate yourself

Learn more about narcissism and how it manifests in people. This can help you understand and deal with narcissists better. By understanding how narcissism manifests in people and the impact it can have on others, you can better recognize the behaviors and patterns of narcissists and develop strategies for coping with them.

Reading books and articles on narcissism is one approach to educate yourself. There are several materials available to assist you in understanding the psychology of narcissism, how it develops, and how it affects relationships. You can also seek help from support groups or counseling to cope with the consequences of narcissistic abuse.

When working with narcissists, it's equally critical to be conscious of your own weaknesses and triggers. To acquire influence over you, narcissists may try to exploit your flaws and manipulate your emotions. You may shield yourself against the narcissist's deception by identifying your own weaknesses and obtaining help from reputable sources.

Another important aspect of educating yourself about narcissism is to be aware of the different types of narcissistic personalities. There are several different subtypes of narcissism, each with their own set of characteristics and behaviors. By understanding the different types of narcissists, you can better recognize their behaviors and develop strategies for coping with them. Dealing with a narcissist can be challenging and emotionally draining, but by educating yourself and developing strategies for coping, you can protect yourself from their manipulation and maintain your own sense of reality and self-worth.

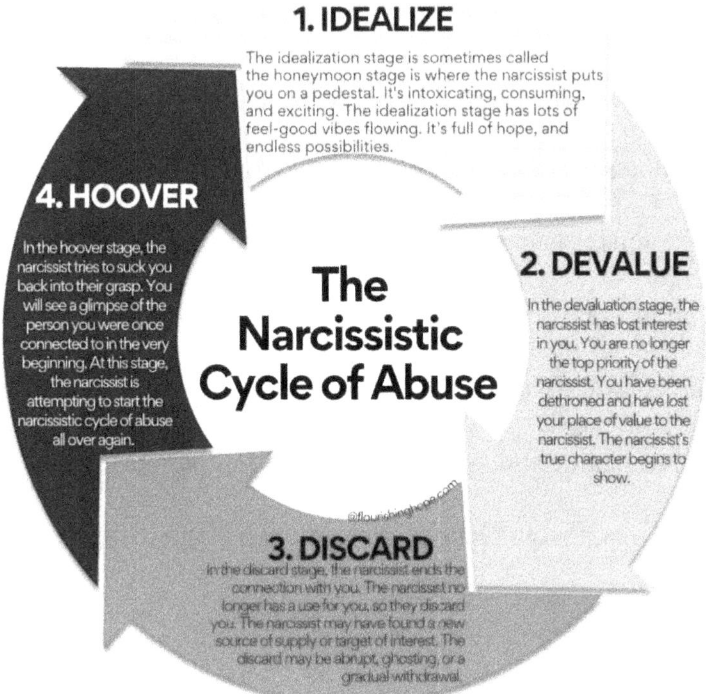

The
Narcissistic
Cycle of Abuse

1. IDEALIZE
The idealization stage is sometimes called the honeymoon stage is where the narcissist puts you on a pedestal. It's intoxicating, consuming, and exciting. The idealization stage has lots of feel-good vibes flowing. It's full of hope, and endless possibilities.

2. DEVALUE
In the devaluation stage, the narcissist has lost interest in you. You are no longer the top priority of the narcissist. You have been dethroned and have lost your place of value to the narcissist. The narcissist's true character begins to show.

3. DISCARD
In the discard stage, the narcissist ends the connection with you. The narcissist no longer has a use for you, so they discard you. The narcissist may have found a new source of supply or target of interest. The discard may be abrupt, ghosting, or a gradual withdrawal.

4. HOOVER
In the hoover stage, the narcissist tries to suck you back into their grasp. You will see a glimpse of the person you were once connected to in the very beginning. At this stage, the narcissist is attempting to start the narcissistic cycle of abuse all over again.

@flourishinghope.com

Flourishing Hope Counseling, PLLC | @flourishinghope.com

Seek support

Going through narcissistic abuse can be emotionally draining, therefore seeking support from friends, family, or a therapist is something you shouldn't hesitate to do. seeking support is an important aspect of dealing with a narcissist. Narcissistic abuse can have a significant impact on your mental health and wellbeing, and it's important to have a support system in place to help you cope with the effects.

Friends and family can be a valuable source of support when dealing with a narcissist. They can offer a listening ear, provide emotional support, and help you maintain perspective on the situation. It's important to reach out to trusted individuals who understand the dynamics of narcissistic abuse and can offer non-judgmental support.

Therapy can also be an effective way to cope with the effects of narcissistic abuse. A therapist can provide a safe and supportive space to explore your feelings and experiences, develop coping strategies, and work through any trauma or emotional wounds that may have resulted from the abuse. In addition to seeking support from others, it's important to prioritize self-care when dealing with a narcissist. This can include engaging in activities that bring you joy, practicing mindfulness and meditation, and taking care of your physical health through exercise, proper nutrition, and adequate rest.

CHAPTER 9

Therapeutic Approaches for dealing with Narcissistic abuse.

The aftermath of narcissistic abuse can be a challenging and complex process. Fortunately, there are several therapeutic approaches that can help individuals heal and recover from the trauma of narcissistic abuse. Here are a few examples:

1. **Trauma-focused therapy:** Trauma-focused therapy is a type of therapy that is specifically designed to help individuals recover from trauma. This approach can be especially effective for individuals who have experienced narcissistic abuse, as it can help them process the emotions and experiences that have been suppressed or invalidated. Trauma-focused therapy can involve a range of techniques, including cognitive-behavioral therapy, exposure therapy, and eye movement desensitization and reprocessing

(EMDR).

2. **Mindfulness-based therapy:** Mindfulness-based therapies, such as mindfulness-based stress reduction (MBSR) and mindfulness-based cognitive therapy (MBCT), can be effective for individuals who have experienced narcissistic abuse. These approaches can help individuals become more aware of their thoughts, feelings, and bodily sensations, which can help them better regulate their emotions and reduce symptoms of anxiety and depression.

3. **Dialectical behavior therapy (DBT):** DBT is a type of therapy that combines elements of cognitive-behavioral therapy and mindfulness-based therapy. This approach can be effective for individuals who struggle with intense emotions, self-destructive behavior, and difficulty in relationships. DBT can

help individuals develop skills for emotional regulation, distress tolerance, and interpersonal effectiveness.

4. **Support groups:** Joining a support group can be a helpful way for individuals to connect with others who have experienced narcissistic abuse. Support groups can provide a safe space for individuals to share their experiences, receive validation and support, and learn coping skills.

5. **Psychoeducation:** Learning about narcissistic abuse and its effects can be an important part of the healing process. Psychoeducation can help individuals better understand their experiences, identify patterns of behavior and thought that may be contributing to their difficulties, and learn strategies for coping and healing.

6. **Psychodynamic therapy:** Psychodynamic therapy is a type of therapy that focuses on exploring unconscious patterns and conflicts that may be contributing to an individual's difficulties. This approach can be helpful for individuals who have experienced narcissistic abuse, as it can help them gain insight into their relationships and how their experiences have shaped their sense of self.

7. **Acceptance and commitment therapy (ACT):** ACT is a type of therapy that focuses on developing acceptance and mindfulness skills, as well as clarifying personal values and goals. This approach can be helpful for individuals who have experienced narcissistic abuse, as it can help them focus on what is most important to them and develop skills for living a fulfilling life despite their experiences.

8. **Creative therapies**: Creative therapies, such as art therapy, music therapy, or dance/movement therapy, can be helpful for individuals who have experienced narcissistic abuse. These approaches can provide a safe and nonverbal way to express emotions, reduce stress, and increase self-awareness.

9. **Cognitive processing therapy (CPT)**: CPT is a type of therapy that focuses on helping individuals identify and challenge negative thoughts and beliefs related to their traumatic experiences. This approach can be helpful for individuals who have experienced narcissistic abuse, as it can help them reframe their experiences in a more positive and empowering way.

10. **Body-based therapies**: Body-based therapies, such as somatic experiencing or sensorimotor psychotherapy, can be helpful for individuals who have experienced narcissistic abuse. These

approaches focus on the body's physical sensations and reactions to trauma, and can help individuals release tension and trauma stored in the body.

Signs of Narcissistic Abuse

1. Love bombing followed by devaluation. Intense praise followed by verbal abuse.

2. Gaslighting: making you disbelieve reality or feel like you're losing your grasp on reality.

3. Intentionally sabotaging friendships or other relationships.

4. Making you the enemy or bad guy for having feelings and reactions.

5. Constant lying to avoid responsibility.

6. Never being at fault for any issues in the relationship. Turning all of the blame toward you.

7. Having a lack of interest in who you are as a person.

8. A huge sense of entitlement. You owe them everything.

Read more on BlessingManifesting

CHAPTER 10

Closing Thoughts

Individuals with narcissistic tendencies are not inherently evil or irredeemable. Like any other human being, they can undergo personal growth and transformation as a result of certain situations or experiences. Therefore, we ought to understand that, there is the need to go as far as helping those with narcissistic tendencies who are willing to change from such diabolical states of being.

By understanding and Making use of the below listed mechanisms, one can reach a mile stone in dealing with narcissistic tendencies.

Understanding Narcissism: Narcissism, in its pathological form, as said earlier is characterized by an excessive sense of self-importance, a lack of empathy, and a constant need for admiration and attention. Narcissistic individuals often exhibit manipulative and self-centered behaviors that can harm those around them. However, it is crucial to acknowledge that narcissism exists on a spectrum, and not all individuals with narcissistic traits are malicious or devoid of the capacity for change.

The Potential for Change: Human beings are capable of growth and transformation, and this applies to narcissists as well. While their behavioral patterns may have been deeply ingrained, certain life events or circumstances can serve as catalysts for change. A narcissist may experience a significant personal loss, such as the end of a close relationship or a profound failure, which prompts self-reflection and introspection. These events can shatter their ego-centric worldview, forcing them to confront their own shortcomings and reconsider their behavior.

Empathy as a Transformative Force: Empathy is critical

in promoting personal growth and transformation. When narcissists face the repercussions of their behavior and experience the anguish they have caused others, they may begin to acquire empathy. They can begin to grasp the influence of their actions on people around them via reflection and improved self-awareness. As they attempt to become more compassionate and courteous persons, their increased empathy acts as a tremendous drive for change.

Seeking Professional Help: Changing deeply ingrained patterns of behavior is a challenging task that often requires professional intervention. Narcissists who genuinely desire personal growth may seek therapy or counseling to address their underlying issues. In a therapeutic setting, they can explore the root causes of their narcissism, learn healthier coping mechanisms, and develop emotional intelligence. With the guidance of a skilled therapist, narcissists can gradually unlearn their harmful tendencies and work towards becoming better versions of themselves.

The Role of Supportive Relationships: Positive and supportive relationships can also contribute to the transformation of narcissists. When surrounded by individuals who encourage growth, challenge their behavior, and provide constructive feedback, narcissists have the opportunity to learn and change. Genuine friendships and romantic partnerships can provide a safe space for narcissists to develop healthier relationship dynamics, practice empathy, and cultivate a sense of accountability.

Reference

Cleveland Clinic, (n.d). *narcissistic personality disorder.* Cleveland clinic.

https://my.clevelandclinic.org/health/diseases/9742-narcissistic-personality-disorder

Kritz, F. (December 20th, 2022). *what is narcissicism? causes, diagnosis and treatment.* Everyday health.

https://www.everydayhealth.com/narcissism/

Pederson, T. (March 29th, 2021*). what causes narcissistic personality disorder*? PsychCentral.

https://psychcentral.com/disorders/what-causes-narcissistic-personality-disorder

Mayo Clinic, (n.d). *narcissistic personality disorder in females.* mayoclinic. https://www.mayoclinic.org/diseases-conditions/narcissistic-personality-disorder/symptoms-causes/syc-20366662

Holand, M. (n.d) *male narcissist*. Choosing therapy.

https://www.choosingtherapy.com/male-narcissist/

OTHER BOOKS BY THE AUTHOR

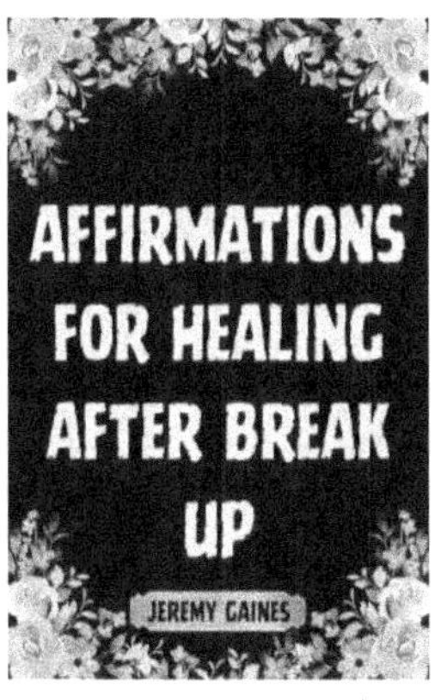

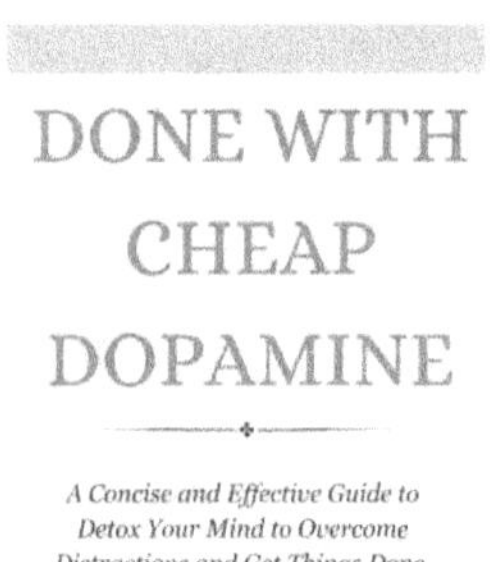

DONE WITH
CHEAP
DOPAMINE
A Concise and Effective Guide to
Detox Your Mind to Overcome
Distractions and Get Things Done.
Updated Version
JEREMY
GAINES

JEREMY GAINES & DR. ZACK SALDERS
THE AI
DOCTOR'S
HANDBOOK
A GLIMPSE INTO
HEALTCARE'S
TOMORROW

Kids
SHORT
STORIES
A JOURNEY
OF FUN AND
ADVENTURE
LILY HENNINGS

9 798328 659505